Signs of Spring

MINDFUL OPTIMISM FOR
MODERN TIMES

LUKE BOYES

Suite 300 - 990 Fort St
Victoria, BC, V8V 3K2
Canada

www.friesenpress.com

Copyright © 2020 by Luke Boyes
First Edition — 2020

All rights reserved.

No part of this publication may be reproduced in any form, or by any means, electronic or mechanical, including photocopying, recording, or any information browsing, storage, or retrieval system, without permission in writing from FriesenPress.

ISBN
978-1-5255-7326-2 (Hardcover)
978-1-5255-7327-9 (Paperback)
978-1-5255-7328-6 (eBook)

1. POETRY, SUBJECTS & THEMES, INSPIRATIONAL & RELIGIOUS

Distributed to the trade by The Ingram Book Company

CONTENTS

Preface
I

Part I: Acknowledge
1

Part II: Light
35

Part III: Warmth
85

Part IV: Growth
131

References
185

THANK YOU

To my family and my soul family, who inspired me to step into my true self with confidence.

To my teachers, who encouraged me along this path.

To those who shine their unique light and help all of us find our loving way.

To all of you, for being here. Thank you.

OFFERING

I have no answers for you
This is my most treasured gift
A clear path lies ahead
An invitation to find your way
My contribution is a promise
To stand by your side
In awe of your every step

PREFACE

Life is a journey of self-discovery. While every individual's path is unique, we walk these trails together. We are all just walking each other home, as Ram Dass so beautifully said (Ram Dass, 2015). There is no one right or wrong way to walk in this life, and no predetermined map to follow. With love, we will all meet each other somewhere along the path, however we may choose to get home. The thoughts and poems in this book are my own traveller's notes thus far. My hope is that you will find them helpful on your journey.

As we walk, we compassionately ACKNOWLEDGE the truth of each moment: the victories, difficulties, and at times outright tragedies that we encounter. In doing so honestly, we illuminate our corner of darkness with our innate divine LIGHT. When we tune into our unique light, we all join together to generate WARMTH that helps nurture the GROWTH of new possibilities for peace, love, abundance, and joy.

The signs of spring are all around us. Acknowledge winter. Shine a light. Feel the warmth. Foster growth. This repeated cycle of life has led us to this very moment. As more of us have begun to see this pattern, the cycle is amplifying. We are the ones we have been waiting for, and this is our time. Our universe flourishes with the contribution of everyone's gift of love, presence, and creativity.

Be kind. Be curious. Be of service. I will see you when we get home.

SIGNS OF SPRING

Spring's subtle flirtation
Begins with soft brush strokes
Upon the wintery landscape

Days stretch out their limbs
Waking from a slumber
And then, the other morning
Did I notice a shift in the light?

But to my mind this cannot yet be
I've been weathered for a time
Mistrusting my soul's assurances

Sensing my hesitation
Chickadees and cardinals sing
So that I might trust
In the promise of summer

PART I:
ACKNOWLEDGE

"'What makes the desert so beautiful,' said the little prince, 'is that it hides a well, somewhere...'"

—Antoine de Saint-Exupéry

PEACE

Today I define myself
By what I am not
And it has become evident
That I am constantly at war
With what is

Peace will arise
When I choose to define myself
By what I am
I Am that, I Am

PATH

The instant I stop fighting
The person I've become
And the path that led me here
Is the moment I become
The person that I am
And choose
The path that I might take

CONVICTION

Conviction is a prison
A false sense of security
Behind unyielding walls
And though righteousness elevates my ego
The bricks stacked ever higher
Build walls just tall enough
To keep me from seeing
A universe of experience

BETTER

It seems so much simpler
To focus on being right
When I pay no mind to my ego
As it fills with venom and pride

When I am mindful
I recognize that I have a choice
To focus instead
On helping each other be better

Let us be wary
Of being so sure of what is right
That we deny that being wrong
Is a beautifully human experience

TO ERR

Be brave
Be vulnerable
Be wrong
Allow others the same courtesy
For it is only human
Yet I so often forget
Wrapped up in myself
And the illusion of absolutes
Clinging to beliefs
As if they were truths
I shame and ridicule
The slightest impurity

A wasteland, uninhabitable
Lies between us
We must meet in the middle
To ensure our survival

Joy, peace, prosperity
All the same in truth
Be brave
Acknowledge one another
And promise
To see the human

GENTRIFY

Any attempt
To improve this place
By shunning some
For the perceived benefit of others
There is no gentle way to say
It improves no place at all

REVENGE

Revenge is a dish
Best not served
The buffet of life
Offers grander selection
To those who choose
To put down their full plate
Upon seeing the potential
Of all the clean tableware
Stacked around the table

ARCHETYPE

Consider
The effort it takes to be bitter
To judge, to hold a grudge

Now
Feel the ease and calm of love
The natural flow it creates

This
Is all the proof I need
That love is our original state

LONG DIVISION

Let us consider
A simple equation

Employing division
To combat division
Results in deeper division

Unity
Is an act of love
That takes any formula
And adds in forgiveness

SEE

It is one thing to not know
A fellow person, animal, plant, or stone
But to not acknowledge their presence
And welcome their magnificence?

To not see each other
Is that deeper pain
We feel today yet cannot name

LEAD

Healing does not ridicule
It does not vilify, or humiliate
Healing seeks to understand
Offers compassion, eases suffering

Deceptively simple,
The healing way
Will test my resolve

I let my heart open
As the Masters did
I lead with love
And trust in what follows

CONSCIOUSNESS

A collective consciousness
Hell bent on pursuing
Full agreement or full stop
Can only perceive and create
An environment equally hell bent
On reflecting chaos and confusion

The intensity with which
We are driven
To divide ourselves
Is surpassed only by the intensity
With which nature is driven
To bring us together

WHOLE

When our lungs burn
When our circulation fails
When our elimination is overwhelmed
When our vision is short
When our nerves are frayed
At what point do we laugh
At the notion we could divide
This whole system
With our imaginary lines?

INCOMPATIBLE

Over a short distance
The arc of a circle
Looks just like
A straight line

Do not be fooled
Cyclical systems
Cannot support
Linear growth

STUCK

Stuck in how things used to be
I imagine myself a dam
Stopping the flow of potential
In the river of how things are

LEAP

What can the fish
Truly know about water
Having not yet made the leap
Through the surface above?

FRAMED

This resisted change
Is frequently framed
As punishment for past sins

Instead, may I see this change
As a unique opportunity
To make peace with the past

And paint a new image of the future

PROJECTION

I can strive to predict future events
With fear and fervour
Or peace and gratitude
And in the balance
I announce to the world
The extent of my faith
In the present moment
And in all there is

CONNECTION

Oh! How we run!
Mentally already at our destination
Or perhaps escaping past events
Thoroughly unaware of this moment
Do our feet even touch the ground?
We cannot tell

Walking mindfully
We feel our heel contact the earth
Rolling through to the ball of our foot
Firmly connected to the present moment
The only destination there is

MISSING

Having happily handed over
The wisdom of my eyes
And the patience of my ears
I might long for the compassion
And the power of my words
That I'd lost along the way
Had I any sense remaining
To notice they'd gone missing

MOON

To the full moon
Goes the glory of the spectacle
But mindfulness helps me recognize the work
That is done in the darkness
Of the new moon

COLD SHOWERS

Having known cold
I can experience warmth

Having known fear
I can experience courage

Having known constriction
I can experience flow

Having known discomfort
I can experience freedom

ADVICE

Don't give advice
That begins with the word don't
Because we don't know
What that don't will do
To discourage the don'tee
Who's been trying to don't so hard
In hopes it might work but it don't

CORRECT

What I love most
About being in the wrong
Is that once I acknowledge it
I am presented with the possibility
To one day be in the right

OVERLOOKED

Having desired
A preferred conclusion
Over all the other options
I have found
That I have overlooked
The most needed outcome
For the greatest good of all

WALK

The task is not to be rid of it
To mask it or sweep it away
The task is to see the love in it
To walk it home every day

OBSTINATE

The only truth is love
An entity beyond definition
Despite our doomed insistence
Through astonishing persistence
To cage that which is boundless

CRAFT DINNER

These are times
Of casual acceptance
Of desperate shortages
In a world of abundance

When I acknowledge this imbalance
I am empowered to choose
To allow the status quo
Or craft a different reality
In every mindful moment

ENOUGH

When I have had the intention
To force abundance
From a place without joy
I have come up empty-handed
Every single time
Yet still I sometimes try

When I have acted with joy
To be of highest service
Within the flow of things
I have found I am always given
More than enough
Yet still I sometimes doubt

WONDERFUL

The child walks by
Dragging a toboggan
While we all stand indoors
Complaining about the snow

IMPERMANENCE

Pacing
Twenty minutes to wait
Four sidewalk squares
In full awareness of winter
The smell and sound of shimmering snow
Mindful footprints in my wake
A sidewalk scraper approaches
As my bus pulls up to the curb
My footprints and I
Are swept away
A winter mandala
Becomes a fresh canvas

POSSIBLE

What if everything
Somehow turns out ok?

What if I don't need
To know how in advance?

What if I was more
Open to the unforeseen?

How might the magic
Of possibility change my life?

PART II:
LIGHT

"Nothing can bring you peace but yourself."

—Ralph Waldo Emerson

VEIL

Angels pierce the veil
Reaching their hand down to ours
Hold true, hold faith
There is always a light
Behind dark clouds

CYCLE

Every drop
Must return
To the ocean

Flowing
Trickle or torrent
Over terrain

Impeded
With patience
Boundaries wear

Stagnant
Evaporate
Condense and start anew

Mother
Judges not the journey
All welcomed home
All free to go

Every drop
Must return
To the ocean

LIGHT

I work so hard
To take flight
To shine bright
Forgetting that
I was born light

My work today
Is to cast aside
These heavy boxes
Carried in from the past
That I hold onto so tight

COMPLETE

I do not seek others
To complete me

What I seek
Are people, places, things
That will remind me

From the moment I crossed the threshold
I have always been complete

FOREVER

From the moment
You were conceived of
As a possibility in this world

From the moment
Of divine singularity
When you first took form

From the moment
You crossed the threshold
And inspired us all

You are forever beautiful

BELIEVE

I seek so desperately
To believe in something
To latch onto anything
When what I truly yearn
To know and believe in
Is myself

SELF

First, learn to know yourself
Only then can you appreciate
How to forget yourself

Temptations abound
These shortcuts to nirvana
Seeking the express route
Exposes part of my story

And then
I am back to step one
The system works

First, learn to know yourself

INSIDE

Silence around me
Is not required
To experience
Quiet within me

PRESENT

This silence
This time alone
Is a gift
A moment
For my soul and I
To commune
To find truth
To breathe
Together

THE NOISE

When I follow
I am led by another's call
I allow their noise to redefine me

Sacred silence defies definition
Home wherever I am
I am that, I am

MANIFEST

I observe where my energy is directed.
Emotions, actions, intentions.

Am I diluting these precious resources,
hastily chasing half-measures?

I must start by seeing where I am, in truth.

I honour the need for quiet and space,
for every-thing is born from no-thing.

Peace of mind is the place from which
soul and self co-create.

Visualizing the path ahead, I name it
to breathe it into life.

I must be true. Be clear. Be simple.

Only then, consistently refocusing
emotions, actions, intentions,
and patiently surrendering to the flow,
do I witness changes around me.

SPECTRUM

From the circling galaxies
To the cycling of atomic stardust
In every cell of our being
Change is life

A fight against change
Is a fight to the death

Facing change
I can choose to project fear
And turn back to old ways

Instead I choose to ask
Is this light?
Where is the light within this?
Can we align our flames
So this light shines brighter?

Find the light
And change everything

IDENTIFICATION

Separate from one thing
Separate from everything

Separate from nothing
I am everything

UNTITLED

Once labelled
Categorized
Placed in a box
It is no longer I
Or so I believe

When I am mindful
I observe my compulsion
To name all things

That is the moment of truth when
I am nameless
I am no one and so
I am one with all things

ELEMENTS

The bell not yet rung
On winter's meditation
I stand upon this bridge

A defiant stream ripples below
With hieroglyphic footprints etched in snow
Proof of past life, perhaps not long ago
Being gently covered by a fresh new coat
So the next civilization might leave its own note

Still
I learn so much
About who I am
From the elements around me

MEDITATION

I sit, as a mighty oak takes root in the earth
I breathe, as ocean waves greet the shore
I think, as clouds form and dissipate
I see, as stars peer into the great beyond
I love, as unconditional as the sun

ATTENTION

My energy flows
Along with my attention
Where does the current take me?
This simple act of noticing
Brings me back to the source
An ocean of stillness and expanse
A place where all is possible

PERSPECTIVE

Some days
I am caught up
In my own waves
And I forget
I am a gentle ripple
In an ocean of stillness

POWER

When everything
Feels out of control
My confused mind
Attempts in vain
To control every transient thing

Taking mindful breaths
I have been inspired to consider
Which elements I truly control

I have come to believe
That there is only one
I am asked to choose my experience
And choose again

The control I seek lies therein

WELCOME

I do not seek out discomfort
I know full well its time will come

When I am mindful I know
To neither shy away nor fight against it
For meeting discomfort with full presence
Is the portal through which I discover
A fully realized self

There is a time to be comfortable
And a time to be challenged
I surrender to the divine scheduling
Of all life experiences

TRAVEL

When a simple song
Can fully transport me
Back to that blessed moment
I must pause to question
What is time, really?

IMMORTAL

As I breathe in
I am inspired
By all who came before me

As I breathe out
I cannot expire
For I nourish generations to come

NOW

When I focus on the end result
I dismiss the miracle that exists
In the flow of moments
In the eternal now

Every breath
Is a portrait in time
And in each moment
I am infinite

REMAIN

Too strong
Structures break
Too weak
Cannot stand

Find the middle path

Flexible and fluid
Though forces press upon me
Cannot deny
I remain

IMMEASURABLE

I stand in a field
Staring at the harvest moon
Wondering how it is possible
That I feel infinitesimal
And infinite
At the same time

HELD

Have you noticed
On cold clear nights
Blanketed by infinite darkness
With nothing but your breath
To prove you're still alive
How the stars seem to shine
A little brighter
As if to say
We will hold your light
And reflect it back to you
Until the sun comes back around again?

PERSONALLY

I am grateful for the moments
When I take something personally
In those moments I can remind myself
I am not the person I think I am

I am grateful for the moments
When I take nothing personally
In those moments I can remind myself
I am everything that is said about me
And so much more

TELL

I rise every morning
And convince myself
That today I will hide
My deepest fears
Yet without fail
I will reveal myself
In subtle and overt ways
To the mindful observer
Through my reaction
To the world's reflection of me

SEARCH

It should be right here
I have looked all around me
Yet I cannot find it

This desperate search
Is at the root
Of such violence and pain

The key to freedom
The path to peace
Is understanding
It cannot be obtained
For it already lies within

SUN

It is no wonder
That I may lash out in fear
Feeling scorched by this reality
All the while forgetting I am the sun

I can only laugh
When I surrender
To all this wonder
I am but a pixel
On a tiny pebble
Spinning around infinity

There is so much I cannot know
I find myself at peace

RELATIVITY

Where I am from
Is not where I am going
But to understand where I am going
I must know where I am from

FOUND

I confess
I have no GPS
And I have felt the unease
Of relying on my own navigation

This is a mindfulness practice
Where I have learned
To prepare for the journey ahead
To be flexible and have backup plans
To slow down
To be mindful of key landmarks
To spot the signs that guide my way
To better identify
My wrong turns
And course-correct with more confidence

Because I have been lost
I know the joy of being found

JUST SO

Initially I believed the ones
Who told me how it should be done
Just so, they'd say

Applying their diverse techniques
I failed spectacularly every week
Or so I'd say

Despite the frustration, I now see
How my practice developed within me
Just so, I say

ASTONISHED

True guidance
Does not tell me what to do
For it cannot know

True guidance
Is but a metaphor
Inspired by nature

It flows through me
And in that moment
I stand astonished

Despite it all
I know where I am

CLEAR

Waves of new information
Wash over me
Being mindful, I am anchored
By my principles
I can observe when I am stirred
By others' agendas
And maintain my footing to prevent
Being swept away

When truth is muddied
By confused messages
There is no need to rush
I send out love, and know I can wait
Allowing time
For the waters to clear

Truth will always reveal itself

HELP SELF

I Am
Lost in my search
Tempted by shortcuts
Elevating the external
Actions become mimicry

I Am
Revealed through service
Reclaiming my precious light
Offering courage and community
Declaring my purpose through being

REALIZED

I am most full-filled when
To the best of my abilities
I ask questions
I listen
I serve

This approach produces
No success
No failure

I can grow naturally
No matter where I am

ENLIGHTEN

I do not wish for your demise
Instead I pray
For the enlightenment of all
Including myself

GURU

My guru
Sleeps in late
Takes a seat
Says few words
Demands much
Expresses little
Tries my patience
Sparks my anger
Amplifies my doubts
Bursts my bubbles
And through this dance
This daily walk on hot coals
I am brought back into the moment
Of blessed unconditional love
And my guru still sits
Unaware of my reverence

THE DANCE

When ugliness arises
I am steadfast in knowing
There must also be beauty
To complete the circle
To dance to the rhythm of life

As mindful beacons of this knowledge
We are beautiful
We see even the faintest glow
Dancing in the darkness

ALL ROADS

The present moment
May feel relentlessly challenging
May feel abundantly joyful
May feel something else completely
Whatever the moment may present
All who approach it mindfully
Will be enlightened

SURRENDER

Having observed nearby flora
I have come to know
That to flourish in this life
I must freely release
A piece of myself
Surrendering every moment
To my full presence
To nature's care
To divine timing

UBIQUITOUS

I had never noticed vervain
Until it was shown to me
And now I see her beauty
Nearly everywhere I go

I sometimes wonder
What other beauty exists
Directly in front of me
That I could only see
If my heart was present enough
To appreciate the spectacle

DEEPEN

I cannot be stagnant
When I stay true to myself

My understanding of self
Deepens with each passing moment
As the flow of mindful presence
Washes away the layers of sand
Upon which I have built my assumptions

BIOHACK

When I believe myself smarter than nature
   I will be humbled by my inadequacy

   When I surrender to nature's wisdom
   I will be humbled by her compassion

STEWARD

I once believed I was an owner
The power of permanence
A sense of reassurance
These thoughts brought me comfort
What I own cannot betray me
Can it?

Time and again I observed
My modern misunderstanding
Out of sync with the natural flow
In a universe indifferent
To contracts and receipts
The things I thought I owned
Were lost to ebbs and flows

It is then that I remembered
In nature, all are stewards
Responsible for every resource
Entrusted to our temporary care

Surrendering to impermanence
I am reassured by earth's abundance

FREE

Were I to live
The way my Creator wants me to live
I would live freely
For my Creator wants for nothing

WEALTH

An investment of time
Spent chasing rainbows
To find a pot of gold

And in return
I have learned
The gold I am to hold
Sits not on distant land
It lies within

My heart has seen
The multitude of colours
Streaming out across the sky
When I share the treasure
Of my authentic self

PART III:
WARMTH

"A human being is a part of the whole called by us 'Universe', a part limited in time and space. He experiences himself, his thoughts and feelings as something separated from the rest — a kind of optical delusion of his consciousness. This delusion is a kind of prison for us, restricting us to our personal desires and to affection for a few persons nearest to us. Our task must be to free ourselves from this prison by widening our circle of compassion to embrace all living creatures and the whole of nature in its beauty."

—Albert Einstein

STEPS

In this life
We find our own feet
Then learn to dance
Together

FELLOWSHIP

Fellow traveller
Our paths have crossed
At this point in time
On our human journey
For reasons we may never know

Consider how highly
The odds were stacked against us!
The alignment of time and space!

To honour this blessing
To recognize this miracle of life
Let us vow to be of service
To the common good
For all of eternity
So we might one day meet again
And celebrate this moment

MORE

We have all been here
In one form or another
Since the beginning

From a primordial stardust stew
And all the miracles that led
To the miracle that is you
Receiving this message today

We are all so much more
Than we believe ourselves to be

BIODIVERSITY

Consider the diversity of people
See the plants and animals, elements and insects
In every measure of earth, water, air
Consider the same intricate balance
In every measure of miracle
That I am

I am
The entire universe
Within this one body
This one body
Is the entire universe
That I am

NEUTRAL

It brings me much joy to know

The Creator of all existence
Is not on my side

The Creator of all existence
Is inside all that exists

Let us be at peace

THE MIDDLE

Denying one
To raise another
Buries both

Right, Left
Connected in the middle
At the heart

Compassion raises, balances
Taking no sides

The wise heart knows
All are needed
All are worthy
There are no sides
In this place of love

DIPLOMACY

In every moment
Of human interaction
I am presented with a choice
To judge perceived differences
Or embrace common experiences
This is the choice
Between war and peace

PARALLELS

We are all the same
We are all so different
We are the truth of life

THOU

No one asked for this
No one needs to be sacrificed
All are to be celebrated
All are sacred
All are holy
None more so than thou

COLORS UPON COLOURS

Nature knows
Diversity is sustainability
Variety is resiliency
And though quarrels occur
All are welcome
All have purpose for being
Nature shows the way

CONSUMPTION

I accept this is all
A sentient manifestation of consciousness
And I understand that we all
Consume one another in the end

Seeing that all is sentient
And all is consumed
Conscious compassion takes only what is needed
Intent on doing the least harm
And seeing all beings thrive

WISDOM

Do lions really believe
That they are kings and queens?

Could it be that the lion
Truly reveres the mosquito
That feeds the birds and small ones
Who distribute and plant the seeds
For the foliage that feeds their prey?

Perhaps there is profound wisdom
In the greater animal world

MARVEL

A tree falls
Seemingly at random
In that moment
An entire forest is reborn

Knowing, yet not understanding
The profundity of small changes
Ignorant of events started well before
And ending well beyond
My time in this place
How can I do anything
But step back and marvel?

I am witness to the interlacing
Of the roots of all eternity

OPPORTUNITY

Everything happens for a reason
But the reason is not what I think

As I adjust the balance
Between logic and heart
I recognize the truth
That each moment presents

The choice to remember
To love and to serve

SANDBAG

We have all the tools
Let us not be complacent
Though the water rises slowly
Its progress is determined

Who among us is present
With a warm heart and worn hands
Stacking one bag after another
To elevate the common good?

ANYWHERE

In order to be of service
I must be fully present
Having nowhere else to be but here
I have discovered
I can be anywhere

DEEDS

A good deed
Born of superiority and anger
Begets equal and opposite resistance

A good deed
Born of humility and peace
Breeds a lasting legacy

SING

The happiest man
That I ever did see
Sweeps the same tile floors
Every day and smiles
While singing the gospel
For no one in particular
Besides himself and his maker

I pray he knows as I do
That in these halls
Though he is surrounded by abundance
There is none more abundant than he

FEELS

Take care of the ones
Whose laughter and joy
Lights up the room
For they are the ones
That feel this whole life most

MAGNIFICENCE

Why, you ask?
I answer, how can I not?
Your magnificence
Shines a light so bright
I cannot help but see you
Through all the cracks in my walls

HEALING

I must tell you
You have a gift
I see it
And name it for you
Despite your humility

Vulnerable together

Healing is being seen
And accepting our full glory

PRESENCE

Humanity's most precious gift
Is to see and hear with the heart

An offering of presence
One miraculous moment
Has the power
To change all of creation

STILL

In that moment of stillness
I could feel your loving presence
From across the globe

I know
That when I return to stillness
You will be there still

GUESTS

What I remember most
About your presence
Is that you were fully present
Your generous light shone
Reminding me
All we need
Is a fleeting moment
To inspire a legacy
That lasts a lifetime
When we surrender to authenticity

SAME

Fundamentally
Elementally
There is no separation
Between us

To fully celebrate
Who I am
I must be eager
To fully celebrate
Who you are

To claim my space
Without denying yours
Is the path of peace
Is true self-love

ACCEPT

I cannot merely tolerate you
To stop there is to ignore
My simmering judgment
Constantly threatening to boil

I must accept you, fellow traveller

You have nothing to prove
The heavy lifting is for me to do
My resistance will fade
I promise you
The instant I remember
To accept myself

AS YOU ARE

Compassion does not feel sorry
Nor does it react with anger

Compassion sees all present
As the miracles they truly are

Compassion knows that from here
We can go anywhere

TRUTH

The greatest truth ever told
Requires only three words
We are love

EXPRESSION

I do not want you to be happy

It is not my right
To impose my desires
And limit your scope

I want you to claim your freedom
To express what emotions you feel
And to do so freely

For true love
Is authentic expression

NO STRINGS

You are always free to leave
Come and go as you will
But I will never abandon you

In tragedy or triumph
I will stand in silent reverence
Without judgment

I love you
I ask nothing in return

CREATION

All that I perceive
Is a reflection
Of my inner state
Our collective choices
And all of consciousness

This is my truth
Do not believe a word I say
I trust you
Find your truth
Bring it to life

In this way
We rise

DIRECTION

I can push them down
And crash alongside

I can raise them up
And rise in return

Same energy investment
I simply choose
The direction of my influence

FORTUNE

There is no better measure
Of my state of inner wealth
Than gauging my reaction
Upon learning of another's
    Turn of fortune

LEVEL

I sometimes fool myself believing
I am ahead of the game or
Somehow above it all

I forget that we are water
We attain a common level
All together as one

STRONG

It has been said
That we are only as strong
As our weakest link

Who are we?
What is strength?
What is weakness?

How we perceive these words is evidenced
By the clarity of our light,
By the expansiveness of our compassion

Let us recognize
That our weakest link
Can be our strength

CLAIMS

None can claim
To be more perfect
Than anyone else
All we ask
Is to join the circle
Where we imagine
A better way
To live this life together
And be better
And better each day

COMMUNITY

There once was a time
To play keepaway with our resources
To hide our gifts out of fear
That time has now passed

The moment has come to stand together
Freed from the struggle against ourselves
So that we may seize this opportunity
To be courageous and see
That when our compassion
Touches even one person
It lights up the universe

STITCH

Step out of the prism
Of all the isms

At the root of the anger
Is a longing for love

Needle and thread
Stitches together
All hearts in the streets

Isms melt away
All are welcome
All are beloved
We move together as one

UNITED

I understand that you are scared
I admit I am too

The terrain changed more quickly
Than anyone expected
We've been pulled into the rapids
I do not blame you for fearing
That we may be dragged into oblivion

You can choose to cling to this old boat
Caught upon the rocky bottom
For as long as you need
But know that this is not the solution
That gets us safely back ashore

We all wait here
We cannot leave you behind
We move as one, united in love

CHANGE

When we are not mindful
Fearful acts
Amplify fear

And if a fearful act
Was met early on
With love?
And if we sought out
Root causes
Rather than fight these ghosts?

Drop those old maps
The way forward has changed
Forge a new path
Know that others will join
Light the way with love

REVELATION

When our heart opens
And we acknowledge magnificence
We can never fully return to fear

This truth scared us
More than anything
And we played small to feel safe
But those days have now passed

With so many open hearts shining
The light reveals the truth
Of what was hiding in the dark
We can no longer look away

SHINE

In our bedazzled world
All fireworks and glitter
The ones who stand out
Shine their own light
Even while reflecting ours

WITHIN

There is no solution to be found out there
It is a house of mirrors where
I cowered in fear of illusions
And was led down false paths
Until the day I remembered to breathe

I became mindful of what is
I saw that this awareness
Allowed these mirrors to serve me
Reflecting solutions found within
Where they had always been

I am grateful for all the mirrors
They help me see what was unseen

PART IV:
GROWTH

"The Tao is constant in non-action
Yet there is nothing it does not do
If the sovereign can hold on to this
All things shall transform themselves"

—Lao Tzu

CREATOR

A post-bang cloud of chaos and nothing
Coalesced into particles
That organized into planets and systems
That had the specific proportions of elements
To build at least one atmosphere and ecosystem
That allowed those elements to agree
To be consistently yet uniquely packaged
Into landscapes and flora and fauna
Of various sentient degrees
With their fundamental elements
In constant motion
And always recycling themselves
To the point where we have been and breathed
Every person and thing that has ever been and breathed
And none of that "formedness" ever seems to unravel
Even though there is no apparent reason
For all these precarious elements to hold together
Except to experience life here, together
And this, to me, is the most beautiful story ever told
I am in awe of our family history

THE SYSTEM

The Creator of all things
Does not want

There is
No punishment
No reward

Only reflection
Only love

SUPPORTED

Did you not believe that Creation
Would provide all that was needed
For you to surrender into love?

That is her soul purpose

EVERYTHING

There is more space
Within all that matters
Than any perceptible thing

Yet, to many
The matter seems to matter most

What changes if we
Direct more energy
To exploring the things
That don't matter?

CHAOS

Love organizes
Outside of time

Patterns undiscerned
Condensing, coalescing
In this moment

What seems to be chaos
Brings truth
Yet to be revealed
On the divine schedule

RHYTHM

Where there is life
There must be music
There is a rhythm
To every living thing

CONDUIT

Miracles are possible
With love
Through us

THANK YOU

Gratitude
Signals to all of Creation
That I recognize her contribution
To the abundance of life

Creation
Having a singular purpose
Can do nothing less than respond
With grander creation

BLESSED

To see the beauty
Of all Creation
In a dandelion in the grass
Is to be blessed
With a lifetime of roses

NATURE

Human nature
Is nature
I turn to her
I remember who I am
And how to be

BODY

Blessed with the inability
To produce essential nourishment
I am blissfully enmeshed
With the environment around me

May I recognize my planetary body
And reaffirm my choice each day
To care for it with as much kindness
As I do in this relationship with myself

THE WAIT

Nature does not hurry
There is a time and place for all things
And at that precise moment
Nature shows us how to proceed
With full force and commitment
Knowing no other outcome
Could possibly be
With the confidence to take
Every second or millennia
Necessary to achieve her objective

Appreciate the difference
Between hurry and focused energy
When this truth is understood
Achievements will spring up
In the flow of all things

GROWTH

New leaf bud
Insistent
Despite the hesitant
Unsure spring

A new leaf
Can only be what it is
Trusting summer
To be what it is
In due time

Growth is trust

ARRIVE

Have you ever noticed
The waves of colour
In the tall grass?
The variety of wildflowers
By the roadside?
Stick to the speed limit
Just for a moment
And know
That wherever you may go
You will arrive on time
More enriched from the journey
Than any reward at the destination

UNSEEN

What is above ground
May whither for a moment

But a strong root system
Nurtured over time
Will provide resilience
A long-term chance
At resurgent life

Nature cares dearly
For the subtle unseen

BOUNTY

After a steady rain
It takes but a moment of light
To produce bountiful growth

TRUST

Weeds grow
And weeds are cut down

When cut
Without mindfulness
Their gift is lost

Observe the process
See the love
See the beauty

Nature balances all things
There is wisdom

SERVICE

When pulling out weeds
I recognize their service
Fixing nutrients to the soil
Preparing the land for rebirth
And, as their final act,
Drawing my attention to the beauty
Freely growing upon the land

I remove the weeds, yes
But I know to do so humbly
With love and appreciation

NATURALLY

Might I suggest
Rather than planting around them
And imploring them to change their ways
We finally pull these weeds by the roots
Carefully and with love
And take the time needed
To tend to the earth
To plant and nurture the seeds
That will flourish
Into the garden of our dreams

WORK

Do the work
Not to be seen doing it
Not to reap rewards from it
Not to find status in it
Do the work simply
Because there is work to be done

TIMING

There is a time for subtle
There is a time for direct
Now is the time
To appreciate the difference

POSITIVE

Let us not fool ourselves
With superficial positive thinking

Call it what it is

Be truthful in identification
And discover the positive aspect
That surely lies within

This is the fundamental step
In manifesting the solution
We will all find
To be positive

BEGIN

Approach the problem
With a beginner's mind
There is no shame in this
I will join you there
You will not be alone

Cleansed of the poisons
Of others' fearful notions
Let us close our eyes
Listen to the words
Feel the intentions
Connect with the heart

This is the singularity
Accessible with every breath
Where all things are possible
We can recreate our world together
In alignment with love

Looking inwards, we see clearly
We have wanted this our whole lives
This moment of love was here all along
We just had to be mindful enough
To begin again

LEGACY

When I am mindful
I understand that this moment
Includes every moment prior
And every moment yet to come

Being aligned with this moment
I cherish both past and future

Approaching life from this perspective
I am blessed with a moment of clarity
That there is a timeless legacy
In each fleeting moment

TIMELINE

I dig fervently into the past
So that I might come face to face with the present
And be empowered to create an enlightened future

FAITH

True faith is a profound love
That encourages curiosity
Maintains equanimity in debate
Relishes differing opinions
Has no agenda to convince
And allows the time to find truth

Because time, like love, is eternal
Accessible to all
Who come to know their true nature

THE SECRET

When true confidence enters the room
It is quiet, humble, patient, trusting
Having none of the answers
Yet carrying an inner knowing
Understanding there is a lesson
In every experience
And, that come joy or pain,
The lesson will shine through
To shape a more resilient individual
And a more enlightened community

ALL WAYS

There is no easy way
There is only the way
The ease of which
Depends on my approach
To the path beneath my feet
And the landscape that surrounds

ADAPT

The terrain changes daily
In this modern world
And I rise each morning
Unsteady on my feet

Stepping into this present
I grasp for the past
To feel safe and assured
But those old guides
Will lead me astray

Modern skills are needed
In this new era of cartography
Awareness to start fresh daily
Flexibility to adapt to change
Intuition from observation
And taking mindful steps
Rooted in peaceful presence

TEMPEST

The tempest
Attracts much attention
Yet it cannot sustain itself
And I know
In time I will find it
Lying peacefully
At my feet

SPACE

Speak
Not to fill space
But to complement it
As a subtle brush
Adds depth
To a masterpiece

Allow space

In words and deeds
This is the way

PAUSE

When the trying stops
Change has space to occur
In harmony with what is

NOTHING

How abundant is this place
When I embrace each day
Expecting nothing!

I am worthy of miracles
Yet demand no such thing
I need not pick fruit
Already cradled in my hand

Free to observe
I see untold miracles
All around
In each moment
From the body's smallest cell
To the auroras above

Seeking nothing
I am separate from nothing

REMEMBER

Reflection of perception all around

Ye are gods
They reminded us
Not so long ago

Do you doubt this?
Claim your faith
Take a moment
Look around
Truly see
And create what you will

MISSION

One simple act
Repeated consistently
Is all it takes to change the world

Wherever you are at this moment
Find your unique way
To leave this place
Just a little bit better
Than it was when you first arrived

THE POINT

With every breath
I am gifted the opportunity to declare
Who I truly am as an individual
And we, as a community
In response to each moment

Perfection is never demanded
The point is simply the choice

Who am I, really?
How do I relate to all of this?
I choose, and choose again
With every breath

BUILD

The road I travel is smooth
But there is construction to come—
This is nature's law

Birth, growth, decline
Seeing this cycle in all things
I appreciate what is done
And acknowledge every transitory pause
With gratitude for the moment
And the journey that led us here

Because I surrender
To the constancy of change
I choose to be a willing co-creator
In every moment of my experience

HOME

Life's foundation
Is constant change

The stability I seek
Arises not from external sources
It is carried within the soul
My lighthouse during any storm

As I return to the soul
I discover the internal truth
That no matter where I am
I will never leave home

CULTURE

In a culture of fear it follows
That faster, higher, stronger, bigger
Are the ideals to which we must aspire
To delay impending doom

We will know we have shifted
Toward a culture of love
When our ideals align
With patience, flexibility, surrender, compassion
Trusting in Gaia to provide
As she has for all our relations

GIVE AND TAKE

What I take from life
Can only be contained
In the palms of my hands
I grasp for more
Dropping what I held before

What I give to life
Stretches out to infinity
Orbiting back to meet and exceed
Every fundamental need
For myself and all humanity

WAVES

Failure
As meaningless as victory
Ebbs and flows

I long not for a lost drop
While swimming in the ocean

Be patient
Rejoice
There is more to come

SIMPLE

Reward is unnecessary
Failure is illusion
Scarcity is falsehood

To be and to love
Is all there is
And there is more than enough
For everyone

See
Joy was there all along

THE SHIFT

What makes me happy
Ebbs and flows
Perpetual highs and lows
What makes me happy comes and goes

Later, I discovered joy
Carried deep within
Never boasting
Accessible anytime
In service to all
And in all I do

What makes me happy comes and goes
But joy reclaimed just grows and grows

GOOD

Good nourishment
May not be appetizing
On the first taste
It does not need to be
Not any longer

Being mindful
I stay open to the good
Long enough to allow
Her full flavour to unfold

I know the good
Will always find me

MEDICINE

The medicine is so beautiful
So loving
She enters only when invited
Some deny
Some poke fun at her expense
Yet still
She waits for them to open the door
None spared
All are healed in due time

UNSTOPPABLE

Pave it over
Try as I might
Fence it in if I must
Love needs only
A beam of light
A sliver of space
To produce a mighty oak

SAY I

To transform "love you" into "I love you"
Is to amplify love
To focus love's infinite depth and breadth
To have the courage
To change the world
In the blink of an I

UNDERESTIMATED

The power of gentleness
The strength of weakness
The success of failure
The reward of doing nothing
The depth of simplicity
The timelessness of waiting
The rippling of stillness
The echo of quiet
The wisdom of not knowing
The beauty of imperfection

CODE

Abundance is simple
Joy is expression
Peace is present
Love is all

"Spring has come again. The Earth is
Like a child that has learned to recite a poem;
No, -many, many...And for the difficulty
Of learning them now, the prize is bestowed."

—Rainer Maria Rilke

REFERENCES

de Saint-Exupéry, A. (1995). *The Little Prince*. Wordsworth Editions.

Emerson, R. W. (1993). *Self-Reliance and Other Essays*. Dover Thrift Editions.

Lao Tzu. *Tao Te Ching Online Translation* (D. Lin, Trans.). Retrieved from https://taoism.net/tao/tao-te-ching-online-translation/.

Ram Dass. (2015, April 2). Ram Dass Quotes. Retrieved from https://www.ramdass.org/ram-dass-quotes/.

Rilke, R. M. (1923). *The Sonnets to Orpheus, Book 1, Number 21* (R. Temple, Trans.). Retrieved from https://www.sonnetstoorpheus.com/book1_21.html.

Sullivan, W. (1972, March 29). The Einstein Papers. A man of Many Parts. *The New York Times*. Retrieved from https://www.nytimes.com/1972/03/29/archives/the-einstein-papers-a-man-of-many-parts-the-einstein-papers-man-of.html.

CPSIA information can be obtained
at www.ICGtesting.com
Printed in the USA
BVHW030839111020
590657BV00005B/36